AF422008

Magic and Wonder and Selected Poems

by Vincent Visco

RoseDog Books

PITTSBURGH, PENNSYLVANIA 15238

The contents of this work including, but not limited to, the accuracy of events, people, and places depicted; opinions expressed; permission to use previously published materials included; and any advice given or actions advocated are solely the responsibility of the author, who assumes all liability for said work and indemnifies the publisher against any claims stemming from publication of the work.

All Rights Reserved
Copyright © 2023 by Vincent Visco

No part of this book may be reproduced or transmitted, downloaded, distributed, reverse engineered, or stored in or introduced into any information storage and retrieval system, in any form or by any means, including photocopying and recording, whether electronic or mechanical, now known or hereinafter invented without permission in writing from the publisher.

RoseDog Books
585 Alpha Drive, Suite 103
Pittsburgh, PA 15238
Visit our website at *www.rosedogbookstore.com*

ISBN:979-8-89027-147-1
eISBN: 979-8-89027-645-2

For Elizabeth, my wife, who is not only my primary muse but also the main guiding force throughout my life which has led me to this fulfilment.

CONTENTS

&

ANNOTATIONS

Those words, phrases and
peculiar pictures
on the left hand pages
reminding us how little we understand,
especially of Shakespeare.

Immediately on page one
we are warned that there is no way
we will comprehend what is to follow
and yet we continue.
Ignorance isn't so blissful.

And do these words sound
different on stage?
I've never seen a blackboard,
stage left, listing words
the audience couldn't possibly understand.

Or were Elizabethans so much smarter
developing a secret language
just to get a good laugh
knowing someone four hundred years later
would never get the joke.

Why not keep just the annotations

and remove the text?
Better yet have the guy who
writes the annotations just rewrite the play.
Oh, I forgot we leave it to Hollywood
to ruin the printed word.

Alas, there is something sacred
about words written to fit the past
yet so hard to apply to the future
like Declarations, Proclamations, Edicts and Credos
intended to answer questions, settle disputes
even end wars, just to make life better.

But it never works!
Being written makes it subject to interpretation
So everyone can apply the meaning that suits them.
Annotations are proof that Language is always changing
But Life is evidence that Human Nature remains the same.

A SUCKER'S BET

In my neighborhood it started early.
Summer days too hot for most activities
we pitched pennies against a cold red brick
wall of an abandoned building with
money from Coke bottle deposits

Or flipping baseball cards using
ones we had doubles of trying
to get the elusive Mickey Mantle.
Winning was everything, walking away
with a bulging pocket of copper treasure
or a stack of cards valueless
once baseball season was over.

The church was an enabler with
the annual springtime bazar.
The loud thwacking of the huge
wheel and rubber arrow luring us.
Hearts pounding, bodies contorting
to urge your number one more space
to win a useless stuffed animal good
only to score points with some cute Debbie.

Teen summer nights spent on the stoop
Playing three card Monty passing
Around a bottle of Ripple.

Nickel and dime pots never
amounting to more than
the cost of another bottle.
Then the turning point.

Either the distraction of the
occasional harmless low stakes
Poker night with beer, stale
chips and dirty jokes, tribal.
Answering the primal need of comradeship
or maybe the tug of a one armed bandit.

Or it morphed into a distortion.
Certain of having developed a talent
to branch out into horse and sports betting.
Getting lost in the Daily Racing Form
scouring the horse's history for the
one word denoting a sure thing.

Believing they've become handicappers
when the only handicap was betting itself.
Then moving on to the loud noise
and acrid stench of casino culture zombies
deluding themselves with " it's just for fun."

Forget about being a fan only
choosing a team to cover the
spread of any sporting event.
A bane to the sports purist
with point shaving and bogus injuries

creating a corrupted trust of every athlete

Hording rent and bill money for trips
to a plastic neon city in the desert or the
run down boardwalk world on the Jersey shore.
Be better to go all the way heading to Monte Carlo
with clothing optional beaches.

These Oedipal fools trying to conquer fate.
A sucker's bet and a bookie's delight
of a hundred to one shot sure to fail.
Unable to extricate themselves
from the tangled web they've woven
right up to trying to beat death.
Only to wind up joining Sisyphus
in his eternal tormenting toil.

AN ANALOG LIFE

Vincent Visco

What's new is old in
a digital life of endless
unnecessary upgraded devices
meant to speed up life
hurrying us to our Freudian graves.

No matter how much faster
they say it will take you,
the planet will still take
twenty four hours to rotate.
Seasons will continue to pass at
the same pace regardless.

Leaving us bumping into
each other frantically reaching for
more, fearing to be left behind.
This from a creature that took
three million years to evolve.

All this has done is to
leave us bereft of our senses.
Gone is the greeting handshake
 or embrace, even a kiss when permitted.
Lost is the telephone voice
 that can't mask sincerity

only senseless communications
with Siri and Alexa. Oh! and
thank you for obese children
lacking in social skills.
Patience has shown us there will be
" a time to every purpose under heaven"

Rise up! Bring back an analog life.
The simple natural rhythm of tick tock,
that heartbeat of sanity.
Post a letter to a friend
in that cursive writing, an
 undecipherable code reserved for adults.
Then hug a person instead of a tree.
So if you want me, call me.
I'll be outside checking
the time on my sundial.

A PIGEON'S RANT

God like in our ubiquity
so watch it.
Stop feeding us and we won't mess up
your statues or you for that matter.
No need getting up early for some worm
with the daily buffet banquet
left for us on sidewalks.
And you say we're dirty creatures.

Unlike those denizens of dumps, seagulls
protected even when taking down airplanes.
Admiring old man abandoned by child and grandchild,
opting to live with flamingos somewhere,
who has adopted and named us tossing out old bread.

Privacy is tantamount,
Never seeing one of our eggs or chicks.
It's always, " look at the pretty robin's egg."
Yeah, until those yammering hatchlings wake you
at four in the morning.
Who says a Coo isn't melodious,
Only cardinals can sing?
We are the fowl crooners
attired in our best Johnny Cash.

Migrate?
Tried it once and left a talon in the door
of the Port Authority bus terminal.
Instead, it's just cold stone bed
down to the asphalt jungle.
Who needs trees?
Distance is our only problem.
With this damn bobbing, it's all a guessing game
that usually ends with disappointment.

Magical we are.
Just ask the disappointed driver looking in the rear-view mirror
expecting carnage of blood and feathers
after passing in front of him.
That's my favorite even though I should be outraged.
What for?
I'll just rise above your mundane existence and spread

   Some
      Good
         Luck

❧

Autumn Moon

Having forgotten to set the clock back again,
he appears in the western morning sky
 for a few hours way past his appointed watch
often going unnoticed, just a bump in the clouds.

Not quite full, still a little shy.
A curious witness to the frenetic daytime
activities, such orchestrated lunacy
and feeling a little dull blending with the blue curtain.

Happy to see her nocturnal prodigal brother
Sister Sun's warmth during these rare moments
takes away his usual cold demeanor, but not
too much for such a pale complexion.

Then just like that, he's gone
Like a miscast actor quickly exiting
this solar stage with a greater
appreciation for the quiet calm of night.

Preferring his roles as nautical navigator and
tidal master with a star speckled backdrop,
embracing his romantic lore that can turn
man into beast and be a lamplight for lovers.

BIRDERS

Those annoying naturalist Peeping Toms.
Voyeurs of the foulest sort.
God asked Adam to name the animals not stalk them.
Flocking beneath trees and on shorelines
geared up and ready for battle

Aiming their howitzer cameras at their prey.
Shooting in rapid succession while perched or in flight.
Disrupting the natural order of things
their presence scaring off potential meals from field and stream.

Photographing mating rituals, egg laying and hatchings, *pornog-
raphers.*
Not a moment of privacy or peace from dawn to dusk.
Looking to reveal every aviary secret
leaving nothing to the imagination.
Here is where knowledge destroys wonder.
Trying to capture in frames a life meant to be free.
The surprise sighting while strolling along
caught in the mind's eye is so much better.

Once gone, they kick up their talons, take out a deck of cards
laugh, discussing the silly human habits.
"Dumb as Icarus, Oh I can't see you with that clever camouflage."
"Did you see the stupid hat on that woman?"
"I really wanted to swoop down and snatch

that ridiculous toupee from the short guy, warm my eggs
so I don't have to sit all day watching them watch me."
Chirping hysterically almost falling out of the nest.
Then thinking: Birders go home, raise all the shades and curtains.
Open every door for the entire day
and see how you like it!

BOOKSHELVES

A view to life compressed.
Encased in wooden walls within walls.
Beginning as a pile of planks from Pottery Barn
to a skeleton waiting to be fleshed out.
Each book a brick building the image
of who we are or wish to be seen as.

Carefully chosen displaying accumulated knowledge.
Titles that catch the attention
of the passing eye ; Adventures to be taken
Mysteries to be solved, Romances
that will never be experienced outside the binding.
Wonders of science and the universe we'll
never understand but never stop trying.

My world of fiction floats on the
upper shelves from Beowulf through
The middle English of Chaucer to a single
volume of Shakespeare's complete works
never to be read in such small print.
Her non-fiction firmly rooted on
The lower shelves, indisputable facts that
look to the upper shelves with a scowl.

Most are dog-eared in appreciation
as an escape from an uncertain world.

Not just "words, words, words "
as Hamlet points out leafing through,
but a reflection of what man is or could be.

For the non- reader photo books
of a world both beautiful and in turmoil.
Curios and framed photos fill empty spaces
depicting a travelogue of a life well spent.

So much life squeezed
in so small a place.
Just an edited glimpse
at a whole story that
can never be told.

ᴧ

CAUGHT BETWEEN HEAVEN AND EARTH

Use to be a Saturday morning train ride was an excursion
into the city filled with anticipation of some
cultural experience followed by
a well deserved meal at the new trendy hot spot.

Gone are those days.
Now I and we work during
that archaic concept, the weekend.

On the F train
heads buried in adventures, scores or
some sensual pleasure from a bit of gossip
printed in the daily rag
we lose ourselves from the reality of our destinations.

Sitting on hard plastic seats contoured for normal sized bottoms
sliding side to side with each start and stop
instead of painting a white picket fence or
ice skating on a frozen pond miles away from urban concerns.
Here my feet are stuck in last night's coffee stains
when it happens.

They enter from opposite sides of the car
doors and worlds apart.
Street poet to my left
self prescribed evangelist on my right.

Each announcing he is here for us
a captive audience.

The poet rants in expletives
why life truly sucks.
Something I need little convincing of right now.
All the time rhyming his desire
to take back life from the oppressor.
While,
Bible totting preacher proclaims the word
righteously condemning the pursuit of money
we are all currently embarked on
to pay the rent
intoning that the next life will be better.

Moving towards each other
firing away in rapid
volleys of discontent.
Not even head phones could filter out
this verbal tennis match.
Their eyes now shift from us to each other locked
in a cosmic confrontation.

Neither seems ready to relinquish
his control over us.
A showdown.
Passengers anticipating the first blow
after words run out
eager not to prevent it.

But, they breeze past each other

steel pole separating them
unrelenting in their verbosity.
Delancey Street.
Leaving us with, "Have a nice day."
If only we would never run out of words.

_ℒ_

CHRISTMAS 1960

Having reached that milestone of double digits,
now ten entering the world of big kids
anxious as to how things must change.
Halloween passed without trick or treating,
instead chalk socks and egg throwing.
Now starts the time of getting in trouble.

Christmas a major rite of passage.
Anticipating first midnight mass, if I can stay up.
Returning home to open presents
not waiting for the next morning.

No toys, a new football and hopefully
a transistor radio to hold to my ear.
Walking and thinking all this while
all day stories of a plane crash that morning
close to school near Flatbush ave.

Mounting a pile of snow on the corner
looking down Seventh ave. closed to traffic.
Wooden police horses closing streets to pedestrians as well.
Smoke billowing, lights flashing and putrid smell of fuel.
Yet, it seems so far away while the horror
of a dental appointment waiting across the street.

Back home, but no response to "I'm home".

My mother handkerchief to mouth, eyes
riveted on fifteen inch screen, black and white
images of carnage and devastation unending.

That look of incomprehension, a mind unable to cope
 with the effect such an event has on family and friends.
134 dead even two guys selling Christmas trees
for a holiday they'll never celebrate.
Lone survivor, eleven year old Stephen.
Just one year of being a big kid.

Next morning in school we're asked to pray for
Stephen who died that morning in nearby hospital
never to be a teenager, go to high school maybe college.
No building his own family for a future.
All the things I thought just happened.

Only legacy, a commemorative plaque with
 four dimes and five nickels fused in his pocket
hanging on the chapel wall in the hospital.
That Christmas was a blur, New Years passed
 and I decided it's probably better to remain
just a kid for a while longer.

CONEY ISLAND THE LESSON CONTINUES

Each year the lesson that is Brooklyn
 and should be the World
unfolds.

For a brief respite
from chaos and harangue
fueled by indifference and hate,
this oasis of time before and
now shows us how.

Community at play resounding
in the multi-lingual voice
of pleasure.

Squeals, shrills and long wails
pass through smiles
lost in the natural
ebb and flow of a common goal,
Fun.

Sky police admit no clouds
to this makeshift desert
where children respond
in English
to questions in

exotic languages
dodging white waves and
bounding over sand skyscrapers.

Bedouin peddlers hawking wares
in this caravan bazaar
where tulip shaped mango has
replaced the knish
and the pretzel gives way to churros.
Jewelry and commemorative photos
fill a void we never knew existed.

.

So many crowded into this small space
with room to spare and no fear of crossing a line
that can be easily swept away with
the brush of a lazy foot.

No cartographer needed to create
a map preventing the freedom
to feel the warmth of sun
and passion for Joy

CYCLE OF ONE

We enter into a world
of simplicity
basic needs and curiosity
compel us to learn and join.

Blissful ignorance gone
More takes over.

Ambitious goals propel us
through years in a flurry,
still reaching for more
never knowing why.

Collect, clutter, confuse
loosing sight.
reaching the ultimate point of chaos,
Retirement— planning not to plan
preparing to avoid preparations

Remembering to avoid Lear's mistake
living the riddle of the Sphinx.
Just illusions
we won't and will.

Falling back on
"As long as you've got your health."

Then worrying about it.
Am I covered?
Denying and accepting the fear.

Say it ain't so.
Take a deep breath.
Life
slowly returning to
Simplicity
Let it.
Wear wisdom well.
It's becoming

For all of Nature's cycles
are beautiful
in their simplicity

GO SIT ON YOUR OWN STOOP

Now,
it's brownstone, limestone, red brick, tree lined
blah,blah,blah realty jargon
Gaze down the unpopulated street, sterile
like post apocalyptic neatness.
Cold dark windows curtained show no glimmer of life.
Passing them might reveal a light
from a computer or game display.
The rare head in silhouette
always looking down never out.
Doors on this block open up
to file cabinets of folders filled with
Dot matrix lives.
Social networking?
"A great investment"
In what?

Gone
is "Ay, go sit on your own stoop!"
from the eagle eyed widow perched at the window
elbows cushioned by a pillow from the old country.
Directed at two boys immersed in baseball card trading
who respectfully rise undisturbed by this ritual and
move on to the next stoop.
She then raises her chin in recognition
to the other sentinel across the street

she has known for forty years.
Her only other sound comes from a reaction
to the Olympic street trials
that take place all day in ;
stickball, box ball, red light green light,
ring-o-levyo, skellsies and hop scotch.
At night
the twenty minutes to throw out the garbage in the airy way
where laughs can be heard from the card game
in the downstairs apartment.
Each window ablaze in light and color.
Front doors wide open
a final yawn from a day's activities

A body without a soul is a useless shell.

ル

GOOD MORNING WORLD

A practice I've adopted now with no need to rush.
Stepping out into a life unencumbered
greeting the day not directed to
anything or one in particular.

Not to just the red shoulder hawk
in her nest having delivered breakfast.
The cat turns to see if he
is the recipient of my salutation,
having greeted the day hours ago.

Or the dog ball in mouth circling me
appreciative of any attention
especially accompanied by a treat.
All the plants surrounding me
seem indifferent to words
as long as there's sun and water.

The sky will remain teal blue
whether I say it or not.
Oak will continue reaching out
to that same sky regardless.
The palm will still brush its
paint-less stroke with every breeze.

Is it my ego just acknowledging

that the day can continue its process
now that I've entered into it?
Perhaps the warmer climate has
something to do with this appreciation.
Stretching out as I say it allows
me to embrace all that I see.

But the quiet of it all creates
a suspense uncertain what the next
step will bring, unable to avoid
the reality that is the turmoil
mankind continues to provoke, encroaching
on all of this. That is the reason.
Just wanting to know that each
morning I step out its all still there.

GREETINGS FROM A DAUGHTER

I came upon one from Japan
while searching for a football jersey
of a team she now cheers.
They're scattered all through the house
and throughout my life
in drawers, folders, books
being sure to remain undamaged.

From Canada, California, Brooklyn, Jersey
different origins same destination
meant to celebrate events in my life.
But when strung together
depict an episodic adventure tale
of a developing identity
from seed to blossom.

Age four is framed and
accompanied by original art work
marking no special event.
Portraying us jauntily walking a field
disregarding a blazing sun
inches from our heads shining
through a rainbow of pink and orange.

A moustache drawn above my nose, very Picasso
with a simple message

" Dear Dad I Love You"
Of course the y in you is backwards
asserting her independence already
hanging over my desk
a constant inspirational muse.

I thought of collecting them
in some orderly fashion
but I like it this way.
Anytime I try to dig up
something inconsequential
I just might unearth
a real treasure.

With all of them she has trumped
a father's promise at birth
" I'll always be there for you"

which she hasn't forgotten
because no matter where she is
she is always
Right Here.

HISTORY OF THE FUTURE

History like memory is faulty.
Rearranging and shifting events in our minds
blocking out what we wish to forget
questioning the truth over time.

Impossible to chronicle every event so
who gets to choose what is noteworthy?
A board of blustery bearded old men
deciding what we should remember?

Two sides to a coin make it
impossible to be all accurate. Explain
Western expansion to the Native Americans
or cheap labor to the Chinese and black slaves.

Yet " we hold these truths to be self- evident."
A poor teaching tool since we never learn.
Ancient times recorded by the most
fallible and untrustworthy creature, man

Never was nor is all inclusive.
Imagine the Bible, Constitution and
any other dogma issued with a female slant.
How different the world would be.
If Herodotus listened to his wife,
the women waiting for the return

of men from countless wars
would've had plenty to say.

Instead of being culturally shackled
for thousands of years relegated
to cleaning up the mess made by men ruining
the social and physical structure of the planet

Time for women to create
the History of the Future
putting the gray area in what's black and white
offering a new vision before we lose sight.

IF IT'S GREEN IT HAS A CHANCE

Her mantra as she putters around
while tending to her garden
full of color and vibrant life
she has carefully created and now

with serious purpose caring
for all the plantings as if
to speak to each of them of
the life they will live under her care.

She is gentle yet critical
of the amount of water and
sunlight having placed each where
it will sustain maximum growth.

A curious slant to her head
wondering as to the life
expectancy that is associated
with each klatch of growth.

Too often she confronts
unexpected decay and death where
 she was sure it would survive

because it was green and
had a chance, yet the

opportunity never happened.
She leaves the weeding
to him who supported her
efforts with pleasure and pain.

They are the presentment
of the perfect pastoral
good cop bad cop team.

Those close to the ground
Inevitably provide food
for insects, birds and rabbits.

Another extension of the
life she has created
providing sustenance in destruction

proving that death from one thing
provides life for another,
not something to despair.

Her face shaded by
the wide brimmed hat masking
any expression of doubt

about the life she's created.
Happy in her role of caretaker for
a world nature has provided.

ॐ

IMAGINE BEING GOD

It was just a random thought
born out of loneliness, when BANG.
Now, what to do with this mess.
Let it float around for a few
billion years allowing this new
electromagnetism and gravity
play with it, see what they make of it.
Be careful what you wish for.

Not bad at all, very orderly and
there's a spot where some
creatures are moving about.
The bipedal one looks familiar,
Very ingenious but restless
and seemingly never satisfied.
Now they've made me
the subject of myths and legends.

Probably will expect me to make personal
appearances in clouds, the sea even bushes.
They've even asked me to
autograph some stone tablets.
I really don't want to be the eternal babysitter
so, I'll leave them to their own design.

So many pleas and questions.

I may be all knowing but
they can't expect me to
dial up an answer all the time.
So, I must shoulder responsibility
for natural disasters, pestilence and plagues.
On rare occasions be acknowledged
for bounty, beauty and love.
Seems there's a fine line between credit and blame.

Some have given me, not one, but
 two alter egos casting me in a trinity.
May sound confusing to you but
try listening to yourself in three
voices and one is a bird's
Then there are those who
disregard me altogether.
I really don't mind them
since there are no expectations.

But the worst thing is
being reduced to OMG.....SMH
Eternity is so much better after all.
Don't have to deal with time or space.
Sometimes nothing can be a pleasant sound.

❧

JAMAICAN SUNSETS

A global point of contention,
the best sunsets.
From Big Sur to Key West
and all western shores
prideful boasts abound
as if we have something
to do with the staging,
like true impresarios

Here are my two cents,
Jamaican Sunsets.
On the shores of Negril
framed by palm and avocado
the natural easel upon which
this portrait is viewed
each night for tourists and natives
who gather in a hushed silence.

This anxious quiet waiting to hear
a hiss as the sun touches the sea.
Each dip behind a cloud creating
a new spectacle never to be repeated.
Colors confounding artists.

Best viewed from Rick's Café
high atop cliffs meant for diving

or on a boat buoyed
away from resort clamor.
You can almost feel the planet turn
into the horizon with each phase.

Like a drowsy eyelid
dipping into the sea unable
to stay awake much longer.
Till that final blink
that ushers in the night.
Then the once glinting sea
becomes a mirror to the moon.

JANUS

Floating, barely touching the surface
and anchored on the shoreline,
the mangrove is enmeshed in mystery.

From the bay a verdant aviary oasis
but from the muddied land
a tangled mess of gnarled

arthritic limbs contorted every which way.
Impenetrable except to nesting birds
and crabs crawling secretly shielded.

Much like the corrupt politician.
A presentment of benign countenance
cleverly masking insidious intentions.

Buoyed by aimless rhetoric
while mired in self aggrandizement
and a covert maze of selfishness.

So many are lured to the promise
of possibilities like anglers
casting beneath the mangrove

only to be snagged by disappointment
getting hooked on the hidden
root of the problem, greed

∂

KING OF THE HILL

Those days snow was plowed to the corners
 of each block creating giant pillars packed firm
affording opposing forts for snowball fights
or sliding down on cardboard carpets.
But today a venue for King of the Hill.

Rushing home from school changing into
wet worthy clothes enough to stay warm.
Rushing out with the promise to do homework
after dinner, maybe two hours before darkness
no time for trivial matters like books.

Meeting at the base of one mound and at
 an appointed time making a mad dash to the top
pushing each other off individually or false partnerships
Once one makes it to the top, the battle to dethrone ensues.

Each one getting the momentary thrill
of holding the pinnacle of the throne
until pushed or pulled down laughing
all the time, never noticing the cold.

Until he appears, Fat Frankie.
Each neighborhood had one maybe went by
a different name; Tony, Nicky or Louie

but the descriptor still the same.
In his school uniform, being kept
after probably for eating in class, drops
  his school bag makes a beeline for the top.

Little Peteie quickly relinquishing his reign
at the mere sight of this vanquisher.
Once usurped he sits smiling welcoming
any attempt at a coup, solo or army.
The look more of a Buddha than royalty.

Not very good at street sports because
of his size, he relishes these days until
  the only one who could end his reign appears, his mother.

 Armed with sauce spoon, armored in kitchen apron
firing Italian expletives more effective
than slush covered snowballs. He slides down
dodging her attempted joust of the spoon.

Heading straight into the apartment conceding his
punishment, leaning bent over awaiting each whack
but smiling instead of a grimace.The aroma of
chicken cacciatora permeates the kitchen, knowing
he would never be sent to bed without dinner.
A penalty no Italian mother would inflict.

LAS OLAS

Sounds much better in Spanish
Words rolling off the tongue
like a crest curling into foam
while waves could be a hand gesture.
Pulled by the moon lured to
the life giving Mother Nature's placenta
back to our primordial beginnings.
Drawn to the planet's rhythmic pulse
a constant surge, dependable
like the sun rising.

Each ola reshapes the shoreline
carrying nautical passengers to
their final resting place, perhaps adding to the
collection of the head bowed treasure seeker.
Winning the endless game of tag with children's feet
but losing to the sure footed sandpiper.
Erasing any footprint made by man
and maybe humankind someday.

Lullaby to the lazy landlubber
eyes closed buoyed away from life's restraints
afloat to some distant shores.
A last look as the sun melts into
the horizon wanting to remember each beat. Yet,
the sea has moved on and already forgotten us.

MAGIC AND WONDER

It was always my custom
to read aloud to my class
whenever beginning a new work.

The hope was that listening would
spark an interest for students
to pick up where I left off.

Most times it worked so
I would pick out places
where I would continue the

process of reading to them as
a shared experience which
would benefit both the class and me.

It brings to mind where my
love of reading got its start.
My mother always found time to do the same.

I assume she did so with
my brother and sister but I
 can only remember her reading to me

from a huge red leather bound bible
and a small green hard

covered book of short stories.

Sitting by her side listening
to stories from the bible on
shiny pages with vibrant colors

along with pictures to help
understand the story developing.
Never interested in presenting a lesson

just the experience of words
creating pictures in my mind
was enough for her.

The short story book was
a step up without pictures
save the one above the title.

By then words began to
become familiar friends
I would have with me always.

For whatever reasons so
many children never have
this same opportunity.

For them reading is a labor
of necessity, something to
overcome in order to keep up.

The magic and wonder that

words can create will
come to them with effort

but once they have it, they'll
know something is worth having
only if it is worth sharing.

NO REMORSE

The cat seemed incapable of motion
eyes focused on one spot, that
predator look but without action.
Usually the gecko or frog would
be easy prey caught and taunted.
But here hesitation and uncertainty.

I looked in that direction and
he was right to hold back.
A pygmy rattle snake was coiled
behind a plant poised to strike.
Something in his nature told the
cat, this is no play thing.

I first grabbed the cat tossing
him inside, then armed with a walking
stick kept handy for such an occasion
and before it could move I plunged
the stick into the back of the
snake's head holding it in place.

Mouth opened and tail wrapped
around the stick, immobilized
until it went limp. Lifting the stick
and certain it was dead there
was no remorse, almost a feeling

of victory over an ever present evil.

Remembering the A.C. technician
whose hand swelled like a
softball after a bite from one
and the neighbor's dog hospitalized
for three nights from the venom,
afforded me a sense of revenge
especially if this one was the culprit.

The iconic image of the statue of
Mary's foot on the head of the
serpent in Paradise came to mind
and I thought how easy it is
to be conditioned to repel, hate
and want to vanquish that which
we fear and label as evil.

℘

OFF THE GULF

At first it comes intermittently
as if testing its reach.
Then a constant breeze
bouncing off the dark blue
waves of the Gulf of Mexico
embracing the west coast of Florida.

A welcome exhale cooling
and cleaning the thick night air
and the many muddled minds
seeking refuge from their daily toils.
Breathing life back into a world
caught up in the turmoil of man.

Carrying with it the promise of new
life dispersing seeds where it will.
The red shoulder hawk hitches a ride
on the jet stream back to its nest.
It playfully nudges hard oak branches against
soft palm fronds like "star crossed lovers".

Animates the air with its luting song
that speaks to all creatures
preparing them for the night's rest.
Blow drying the fields of grass
from an afternoon down pour

coiffing each blade, a perfect crew cut.

Mixing the remnants of sea salt
with floral and herbal scents
creating its own unique potpourri.
The symphony of leaves rustling
in a soft melody never to be repeated.
A canon carried from tree to tree.

Gluttonous mosquitos having gorged
themselves on strolling dog walkers
drunk and temporarily sated
from their plasma filled feast only
to be whisked onto the banquet table
For dragon flies and lizards alike.

Ultimately dying down to
a whisper that reassures a
return performance, one constant
in an ever uncertain world.
Then tenderly tucking in the evening, renewed
beneath a glinting star speckled canopy

PATHWAYS

Not of stone or sand or
well-worn trodden earth
opposite the one not taken,

but those propelling us to our destiny.
Unseen and formless never straight
always with unsuspected turns.

Detours taking us to a place
we never expected or planned
and yet here we are,

but not for long.
No way to prepare for such
a journey so we submit to it.

Stumbling for a balance between
what we want and what will be.
Turning back is never an option.

That unrelenting human spirit
sure it has a choice in the matter
feeling for a light switch in the darkness.

Continuing on this life long quest
that is more prescribed than chosen

taking each step cautiously uncertain.

Even being surrounded by so many
 it's still a lonesome traveler
looking for destination sign posts.

An unending play beginning with an
empty stage and ending each act exiting
only to return in order to begin the next act
    Over
        and
            Over

PETULANT CHILD

Those moments just before sleep
random thoughts traveling through
space and time flash before us.
Each thought forgetting the previous.

Is the mind searching for something
lost or hidden in the recesses?
Beginning with the day's events then by
association a tableau of unrelated faces and places.

Like the petulant child twisting and
turning in bed refusing to fall asleep.
The mind will not let the body rest
jealous because it can never rest.

Forever operating tirelessly or else
organs shut down committing mental suicide.
Like a shark swimming till it drowns.
Our consciousness reminds us of our shortcomings.

Regrets, longings and missed opportunities.
Should've said this or done that.
Things we want to forget but can't.
Things we want to remember begin to lose form.

Asserting its control of our being allowing
some thoughts to creep into our dreams.
It relents having exhausted the body.
Muscles relax as the corporal world disappears.

PUNCH LINES

When I opened up the box of poetry
and read the directions I noticed
it came equipped with punch lines.
Seems all poems end in some way
with a fragment of sensible thought
that ties together the metaphors and allegory.

Not necessarily a lesson or a moral
but an end to a means created.
When I read poetry I'm always
in suspense as to how I will be
surprised by the poet's last
turn of a phrase." Ah, very clever!"

Shakespeare had those puckish couplets
that turned a sonnet upside down.
Frost's final brush stroke to a landscape.
All of those Odes and Elegies leading
you down a maze that ended in a frozen thought.
Forget Epics, they end with a beginning.

Poor Prufrock wakes only to begin again
and what a surprise when Richard Cory
 puts a bullet in his head unexpectedly.
The last five syllables of a Haiku
always amaze me with their cunning.
So let me see if I can put this thing together now.

SILENT LEAVES

Upside down at the foot of the bed
I am witness to the maelstrom of an autumn wind
through a closed window.
Framed
    in a blue sky
                etched by barren branches.

Clusters of remaining silent leaves mop the sky
of any clouds quietly passing
this delirious dance,
a pantomime from inside.
Play
    or confusion.
One can be mistaken for the other.

Individually
      they fall
           Alone.
From behind glass
it's impossible to hear the cry of one
in particular.
Torn
 from its tree of origin.
A yellow droplet
like a blank post-it that's lost its adhesion.

After so much time perched above
                        the mundane cares of the world
it begins its
            dissent
                    to earth.
No direction or control
just moving by a whim of nature.

I right myself to trace this
noiseless clamor
as it desperately tries to avoid
being grounded
like a disobedient child that has wandered
too far from its parent.

Downed
        it scrapes along the pavement
mingling with others unlike it
along with a page of news print
                        coffee cup
                            and bill of fare from take out
piled on it.
Any moist life left evaporates.

It never knew that
            this is the way it is

ॐ

SPANISH MOSS

Awe struck Brooklyn Boy
immersed in Southern Culture
wearing a child's look of amazement
viewing a variety of vegetation
that defines the South.
Sun and shade create a cocktail
containing every hue of green
replacing the cold gray of
concrete and mortar left behind.

Coffee cup in hand I stand frozen
peering deep into a world so new, yet so old.
With all that I see so much is unseen
covered in layers of life.
But what stands out most prominent
in this lush landscape is the
gray Boa of distinction worn by the Oak,
Spanish Moss, looking more like a decoration
embracing the romance of Southern charm.

But like so many things perception
changes upon closer inspection.
What was lacey is now a lattice
of course fabric, creating a home for parasitic

Chiggers, waiting to attach unsuspected.
At once I'm repulsed retreating
back into the dusk as coffee remains
spill from a tilted cup, disappointed
by Nature's deceptive allure.

Looking back watching the moss
sway in the evening breeze
wonder quickly turns to cynicism
resurrecting Billie's lament, Strange Fruit indeed.
Another linchpin of Southern Lore recalled
deeply rooted in American history.
Transported back to northern sensibilities
a war wages in my mind, "a distracted globe."
Not even the silhouette of a velvet sunset could soften this
image.

But Nature cannot be blamed that
the Oak was forced to share its branch
with the limp limbs of hatred
that human pendant of despair
it could not unclasp.
The epiphytic moss depends on
the tree for its life
where so many lost theirs over
a mass misguided fear of displacement.

Maybe the tree is shedding
elongated tears for what it couldn't prevent.

Its beauty must not be overshadowed
by Man's pernicious past inquisitions.
Standing firm against memory
I will not allow this unalterable
reminder to ruin what is now.
Let Nature stand apart from culture where
so much will never be Gone with the Wind.

❧

STATUE OF BUDDHA, THE THIN ONE

She tells me I should meditate
to ease my stress, in front
of the statue of Buddha

He sits on a butterfly bench
eternally serene with legs folded
hands in cup fashion where rain collects.

Surrounded by flowers and plants
eyes closed. He doesn't know
 the world I see, just what's in his mind.

What am I saying, he's stone
without a mind and I could never
bend my legs like that, more stress builds.

One shoulder drapped next to
a floral necklace and bracelet. Beaded
 hat atop a head with elongated ears

that cannot hear the chimes above
while I hear everything, which I'm told
to block out, but being of flesh and blood

my spirit is trapped in this world.
I can feel the spider that walks

across his chest but he never reacts.

There has to be more common ground
for this to work or I'll wind up telling
 him to wipe that stupid smile off your face.

I'll give it another shot tomorrow
when I might be less corporal. He'll still
be here smirking at my inability of release.

ॐ

STILL LIFE

There's a certain uncertainty
in the stillness of dusk.
Not a leaf or palm frond sways
in this frozen moment.
As if nature is striking a pose
for painters and poets alike.
A view into eternity.

Should it allow the night to
devour the remaining azure pink light
on the horizon, sweeping away
all the colors created in the day.
I'm reluctant to reach for the glass
of wine in this still life
interrupting this picture of perfection.

Everyone experiences these moments.
Imagine indulging ourselves in a collage
of life's perfect images.
A series of captured events
we wish would last forever
returning us to an Eden once lost
however undeserving we've become.
Where night cannot draw the curtain.

SUSCEPTIBILITY

If a person is singing that
usually means the person is happy.
That may not be the case
for a nearby listener
especially if it's the first
thing you hear in the morning.

My wife often wakes rolling
a tune off her tongue or
humming if she forgets the lyrics.
If I wake up to this, it's over.
The power of suggestion on steroids.

That tune is now tattooed on my brain.
If I were to put a water hose
to my ear and try to flush it out
It wouldn't work. Its tentacles already
entrenched on my cerebral cortex.

This morning it's Aretha Franklin's " Respect".
For the rest of the day images of
Aretha from magazines and T.V. will haunt me
along with disjointed lyrics from the song.

At the gym she replaces
the trainer's voice saying

Just a little bit, just a little bit
Paying for a Starbuck's coffee I hear
I'm about to give you all my money

In the car different music is playing
but I know Aretha is lurking
behind the dashboard waiting for me
to exit the car and latch on again.

My dog greets me at the door.
Behind his innocent stare all I hear is
Sock it to me, sock it to me, sock it to me.
My wife approaches smiling
and I want to say
Your kisses are sweeter than honey

But she wouldn't understand
having long forgotten what she
started, her mind a clean slate.
This mistress of torture unwittingly
waiting for the next tune
that will glide through her mind
and plant it in mine after the first yawn.

THE BATHROBE

Hanging on a plastic hook
behind the bathroom door, deflated
a flannel skin without a skeleton.
It's hard to distinguish the arms from the frame
with folds curling into plaid waves.
The only outstanding feature is
a belt hanging down trying not to touch
the cold tile floor.

Its colors, red and green, are
evidence of a Christmas gift
probably meant as a joke
since it wears the label, Victoria's Secret
and was wrapped in that seductive pink striped box
with that naughty black ribbon.

But this is no form fitting bodice
just fuming with arousal.
It has function.
A garment of transition
enveloping the water warmed body
protecting it from the ever present chill
lurking outside the shower stall.

Taking her to the bedroom to be
exchanged for daily togs or

a quick slip under the warm sheets and waiting body.
Then returned moistened and soap scented
to dry and await its next attiring.
It's become parched since its last soaking.
I'm not even sure how it got there.

Was it forgotten or left
as a remembrance?
I could easily dispose of it somehow or
cut it into rags for polishing and dusting.
Such an ignoble end for this
trusty armor of comfort.
It's easier just leaving the door open
cornering it out of sight
till it crumbles like the past.

ペ

THE BLUE DOT

Once while walking the dog
a feeling of being watched
causes me to look over my shoulder.
An unblinking ivory eye spying.

A single light sieving
through naked oak branches.
A celestial pin prick with
no other light visible

Can't be a star, no sparkle.
Then a planet quietly
invading the early evening.
Mars or Venus, no matter

A passing breeze in the trees
momentarily masking its intent.
The stuff of what springs forth
inspiration or curious concern.

Hypnotic and thought provoking
until the night quickly blackens
The whole sky and the Big Dipper
ladles out milky stars

Billions of years coursing through the

the sky making this short life inconsequential
The vastness of it all making one
feel as an inhabitant of a quantum world.

Wondering if out there one peers
out into the night sky seeing a
blue dot while this old planet
groans as it turns night into day

THE DOG'S BUTLER

is what my sister calls me.
Not even Jeeves, just the butler.
This because I fetch his ball which
has errantly or purposely found
its way under the bookshelf or couch
again, which he cannot squeeze under
or behind in order to retrieve it himself.
Then amaze him with what ease I can.

The juxtaposition of dog and master
is fine with me, an Italian retriever.
I don't even realize when I'm doing it.
He'll sit, look at me, bark then look in the direction
 of the ball with another toy in his mouth.
All he wants is to play soccer or futbol
 depending on which side of the Atlantic you live.

Don't mind if I'm told " You spoil your pets."
Oh, there's also a cat involved who
meows outside the bedroom door between
three and four in the morning wanting a snack.
Is life so tedious that I can't afford
 some time to answer their whims?
We could learn much from having
such simple pleasures fill a life
away from the day's toxic news.

Luckily we don't live in dog or cat years.
Their short respite with us should be
the best we can provide and cater to
 without caring about little annoyances.
Why rescue or purchase these creatures
in the first place if not to pamper?
Then there's that way they look at me.
The same way I look up at the stars in the heavens.
I'm everything to them. Quite an honor.

They can't hop on a plane
headed for exotic ports-of- call.
Such places don't exist in their world.
Just this modest coastal home
that affords enough space to be content.
A concept with which people have lost touch.
So, I will continue butlering on,
serve dinner, fetch balls, take on walks
and at night have him curl under my arm
resting his head on my chest and fall
asleep to the lullaby of a heart beat.

THE PAUCITY OF POETRY

Every cultural leap in social evolution is
 accompanied with or spear-headed by Poetry,
the first and foremost Literary genre'.
Civilization was begun through the epics
of Homer and Virgil establishing honor,
role models, codes and a sense of
pride for oneself and country.

The decaying Roman Empire turned
to Dante's Divine Comedy to infuse a
 much needed morality before a collapse.
While Milton's Paradises offered hope
at a time when mankind was struggling
for direction even a blind man could see.

Petrarch and Shakespeare, bookends to the
Renaissance, wrote sonnets that allowed
love to flourish despite plagues
political unrest and religious Reformation.
The Romantics; Byron, Shelley and Keats
showed a Humanism that made
us one with God and the universe.

Wordsworth's warnings went unheeded
while technology continues to suck our souls.
Frost embodied the immortality of nature

and we just selfish visitors who now
lament losing a landscape that
was both beautiful and productive.

Even Eliot's nihilism made us
search for meaning in a Wasteland.
Hughes forced us to confront racism and
social injustice, a lesson poorly learned.

Then it would seem the Muses took
 a vacation leaving a Paucity of Poetry.
The earth continues to spin on its axis
but evolution has halted in its tracks.

Emotion has become a valueless commodity.
We are afraid to feel and have become inured by violence.
The once beauty of language has
been replaced by provocative assaults
and the world has fallen far
from the rhythm of life itself.

Poetry must once again come to the
rescue before we find ourselves
lurking in the shadows of another Stone Age.
Verses are needed to uplift heads
with confused dour expressions,
brighten days that have lost their glimmer
and give back harmony to a world
that has forgotten the lyrics of the Human song.

♲

THE SCENT OF MEMORY

Over time memories take on different dimensions
converging with an olfactory experience senses merge
to present a picture beyond the flat image of a photograph.

The thick summer morning air filled with basil from
a tenement backyard flowing in through a window fan
soon to be added to the Sunday macaroni sauce
being stirred by my mother, the only thing that could
snap me out of a deep sleep from a Saturday night debauchery.
Eyes closed head over pot inhaling a culinary perfume
torn crust of bread waiting to submerge.

The evening embrace of a father home from work doused
in salt sea air coating his longshoreman work clothes.
Remembering my four years of high school
through the smell of academia emanating
from a landmark building filled with antique text books.

That dreary eyed chocolate haze preparing my
toddler son's late night ritual or my
infant daughter's security blanket draped on my shoulder
her head resting in that baby's breath
you wish would last forever.

The fragrance of Jean Patou's Joy on her neck
a sure sign of getting lucky that evening.
Of course the all night aroma of bread from the ovens
of the corner bakery that recalls a life in Brooklyn
If only we could take the next step
And begin tasting memory as well.

$\mathscr{L}$

THE WORLD OF LAZARUS

After the click of the author's pen
or the powering down of the laptop,
that's when the characters' lives
from a novel really get interesting.
Waiting for the author to turn away,

they gather between the lines
critiquing the day's events though
some are too tired after a long
day of trials and tribulations and want
 to remain in suspended animation.

Main characters complain about
not enough plot development to
enhance the image portrayed.
Minor characters just shrug off their
 situation the same as day laborers.

Often they look at each other
suspiciously as if knowing what's
in the mind of the author
not trusting any plot twists
resulting in conflicts they wish to avoid.

Some voice displeasure with the

uncertainty of impending developments
sure they are headed for tragedy but
getting no reassurance from the others
who think " better you than me."

They all look into the void of
the empty pages ahead wondering
what fate has in store for them.
Though making it this far might
mean they will be there at the end.

Then much like Lazarus, unable to
explain where he'd been yet
glad he's not there anymore,
they can only wait in darkness
till resurrected by the author's return.

❧

UNDERGROUND ENTERTAINMENT

Best theater bargain in NYC, the subway.
In the underbelly of the capitol of the theater world
for $2.75 a 24/7 urban travelling minstrel show
plays to the amazement or chagrin
of thousands of riders daily, everyone's a critic.
With a metro card ticket swipe you're there.
In some cases standing room only a captive audience.
Never knowing what performance awaits at each station
and of course tips are always welcomed.

Act 1: Doors open curtain rises.
With the first strident chord and vocals
the Mariachis enter, an 8am. wake up call.
With cowboy hats and boots covered by
their guitars, they compete with the screeching
turns from the train's wheels.
Must sound better at night after a few tequilas.
Finished they bow walking through with
a young boy in tow with outstretched hat.
He should be in school but here
he's learning how to survive.

Act 2: Much needed comic relief
He begins by welcoming us to his living room.
" Like what I've done with it, don't spill any coffee."
Says he's a product of his environment, born on the A train.

Also met his wife on the subway
"should've gotten off the previous stop."
Then a constant stream of one liners, old and new.
Still a tonic for passengers momentarily turning away
from today's news this rainy morning.
Ending with " Please take your trash , I'm expecting more
guests."
No hat here instead a worn out Starbuck's cup.

Act 3 : Something to set the mood.
Three distinguished black men mosey on in snapping
fingers in a cappella, never missing a beat
as they glide through the building crowd .
Gospel , soul or seasonal depends on time of day or year.
A single tune gets you from this station to the next rhythmically
smiling, bowing with fedora upturned still on key.
My station, exiting with them resisting the impulse to chime in.
I climb the stairs knowing I'll have sunshine on
this cloudy day even without my girl.

Intermission : in this case a job
Encore: Return trip

Act 4: Salsa ! every night is Friday night.
Salsero twirls with size blonde puppet attached at toes
moving with the music coming from his belt.
Dolls protruding butt pushing against
work wearied riders side stepping
not wishing to cut in but hard to ignore.
Still the few who join in temporarily ignite
a pulse to this underground artery. A final spin

as puppet's hand reaches out for a tithing.

Act 5 : dumbfounded!
Out of nowhere slight- of- hand magician
spinning wand, top hat placed on folding table
taps, removes and dove appears
flying one end to the other passengers ducking
then returns back on top of the hat.
Bubbles dancing in the air, balls float around rider's heads
How does he do it? Wait, where's the dove?
Waving wand over lady's head then taps the floor below
lifting wand with pair of panties at the tip
Hand to mouth she flusters, then laughs, they're not hers.
Offering the upside down top hat he exits. Where's the dove ?

Finale : Drama
Unseen at first the wheelchair rolls in, legless passenger
wearing his hat of honor, Vietnam Veteran.
No one dares make eye contact looking
for distraction from expected sad story.
Not here. A sermon instead.

" Great to be alive," smiling " I'm here ain't I,
know too many that can't say that."
Train lurches. bodies shift but wheels stay locked.
" I would've given my life so you could be free to ride the train."
Heads turn to focus on what will follow.
" I ask for nothing except to think about making a sacrifice
when you can, we're in this together."
Along with grateful passengers I exit.
One slips a twenty dollar bill in the back slot

of the chair while patting on the shoulder.
Thank you, from all who leave.

Bounding up the stairs, I feel blood coursing through my legs.
Not feeling the cold gray night being propelled
by the exuberance that is Life,
looking forward to a return engagement

WRONG PLACE AND TIME

I can see myself standing on
the walls of Troy spear in hand
glaring down at the Greek army.
Certainly the royal blood of Hector
flows through these heroic veins.

It would suit me fine to be
amidst the noble Medici family
without the plague of course.
Just chatting with Botticelli or cleaning
away scraps of marble for Michelangelo.

The salt air would feel great
sailing with the Spanish Armada but
having nothing to do with the Inquisition.
Just the word swashbuckling is captivating
without being blown away by Sir Francis Drake.

We all have pictured ourselves existing
during a time that seems more suited
to our tastes without the problems
that history reminds us went along.
Just the romance and glory is enough.

Because it's easy when you know,
in hindsight, how things will turn out.

Especially when you know what to avoid
like being sure to stay away from
the haughty doomed court of Louis XVI.

My morning chats at a café
on the serene Left Bank of Paris.
Fraternizing with the Lost Generation,
helping them to find themselves
after nights of endless debauchery.

No doubt I'd do a mean Fox Trot
across a glistening ballroom floor
listening to Tommy Dorsey and Glen Miller
entertaining us while forgetting a war
waging across the Atlantic and Pacific.

Being stuck here and now in
this of all places always makes
Nostalgia gratifying. Those oldies but
goodies and black and white films
seem so detached from reality.

The exercise of transplanting
oneself, escaping to former times
never ends up the way we wish.
No matter where or when we choose, it's
never the right place at the right time.

www.ingramcontent.com/pod-product-compliance
Lightning Source LLC
Chambersburg PA
CBHW061348140726

47997CB00003B/1111